Incandescence

Incandescence

ISBN 9781763825918

Walleah Press
South Launceston
Tasmania, Australia 7249
www.walleahpress.com.au
ralph.wessman@walleahpress.com.au

Incandescence

Susan Austin

Contents

First day falling

in this strange office
where half a tap offers boiling water and the other half chilled

she tries to smile and read name badges
with an imperceptible downward flick of her eyes

new colleagues bear gossip in their arms like kindling
she wants to light a fire to warm her nervous bones

instead she plies the levers on her chair
struggles for equilibrium

she logs in, opens her calendar – blank and questioning
slots pens and paperclips into a plastic caddy

slips away to the bathroom … scares herself in the mirror
with an expression like being lost in snow

or gazing into the sky at night to find God
but only managing to spot a falling star

Dust

what settles on carpets
in a still house

    you weren't sure

but some mornings you watched
the symphony of particles
move in the curtain-slitted sunlight
tried to breathe through your nose

just how your life withered like porotic bones
losing mass inside a moving body

    you weren't sure

not angst or sadness
just the constant chill drizzle of anhedonia

you did try to catch the particles on camera
leaving the film undeveloped on your duchess
as a meaningless memo to posterity

Palliative patient to volunteer

you kindly offer
your talc-pungent time

rolling clouds   under   up   black
you block the window
look at me   I stare back

watch me spit in the bowl
lucky bitch   you don't know when
your time will be up

remote controls   line the chasm
frozen peas   whirlwind minutes
innards wrenching   pain consuming

being sucked down   put the plug in
put the plug in!
fucken help me!
sliding now
damn don't leave me!
storming now

you try to calm and reassure
pill and glass and blood and spit

misplaced ticket
derailed dreams

adjust the blanket

opiate cobweb
caught thoughts wither

like my pulse
you linger
softening
this nauseous infinity

A ticket to transformation

the pill slides down his throat
sticks to the side
          halfway down
he gulps home-brew
knows it won't take long
for worries to fall like confetti
for the snug blanket and couch
to become coffin-like, propelling him to
wander into nearby bush
where trees will jive and shriek
with twisted eucalypt humour

he sits waiting for his senses to ignite
for each ant marching along the windowsill
to become iridescent, a hundred busy gems
for the beetle in the base of the pot plant
to start glowing with a cataclysmic crown of gold

The ring catches and shoots

In the weeks before the wedding she drinks milk –
litres and litres of it –
to strengthen her bones,
fortify her – for what – she's not sure
       is the right path ahead.

If she had a horse she would ride
kilometres every morning,
exfoliate anxiety on vistas and eucalypts
hooves pounding the weed-lined tracks
       around her subdivision.

There are reasons she said yes, of course,
but as she uses her Egyptian brushed-cotton towel
to pat dry bruises after a shower,
       the reasons don't jump out at her.

The ring though
is great for twirling in the queue at Centrelink.
It catches light slicing through the partly-curtained window
and shoots sparkles up
across   the ceiling of sighs.

She savours this chance she's been given
to become a bride –
lacy, milky white,
       celebrated.

Chinchilla

Matching Colorbond fences connect
matching Colorbond houses
in a noughts-and-crosses grid
of perfectly flat, perfectly-turfed allotments.

All around there are new houses, year-old houses,
houses in construction,
rising like button mushrooms
in this mining-boom town.

A hill-billy town, I called it,
upsetting her after I'd flown and driven in
from the bottom of the continent
to see where she'd settled.

Still no Maccas, KFC or Hungry Jacks,
but when the first one comes it'll go off,
become the talk of the town
like when Maryborough got its first set of traffic lights.

Cuddling the new bub in the Ikea chair,
she looks out between the fence and the patio roof
to fluffy white clouds stationary
in a sunny blue sky.

She takes it easy, her only ambition these days —
to be a good mum.
She worries when bub struggles to attach
to her troublesome right breast.

At six months, she and her husband fit in a trip to Brisbane
to play a comeback gig with their punk-rock band.
They belt out songs from their set-list
alternating with nursery rhymes on the long drive back.

She smiles at clucky grandparents on Skype,
pram-pushes around the block with another new mum
before her husband drops in for lunch,
delivering more pastel, size 0 jumpsuits.

Downtown she does baby show-and-tell
for her real-estate agent, banker and butcher,
bumping into others she knows in the street.
Her list of twelve errands ticked off within one hundred metres.

The newsagent prints photos,
stocks make-up, herbal tea,
five stands of fake fingernails
with a coin-operated pony-ride at the front.

The two-dollar shop smells of cigarettes
and we have to bang the bell twice for service.
There are two fashion shops — one for men and one for women —
and it's never any trouble to find a park.

Back home in the evening,
after barbequed steak and vegie burgers,
we sink into the sofa to watch wide-screen TV
wearing 3-D glasses.

A different kind of online

She dreams of upgrading to a bigger boat,
a higher-horsepower outboard.
Files the dream away as she hits the open ocean,
speeds up enough to plane.

Sea-spray short-cuts her to the present,
scanning the ocean in real time
for good places to pause and fish.

The old-fashioned Wi-Fi of winds and tides,
the template of sand-banks and
the stored data of experience logs in.

She throws the anchor out,
casts in a line,
starts spinning the reel when it's made good depth.

Downloads gigabytes of patience.
Rests her finger on the line to monitor the tension,
any hint of a bite.

Clouds congregate,
fish disperse.

Marine-scanning monitors are redundant
when she can screen-shot regularly
with pelagic eyes accustomed to buffering and glare.

She motors around,
exploring different domains.

Catches a Bluetooth tuskfish,
a couple of Banded morwong.

Setting off back home
as the sun compresses itself
against the singed horizon,

it's the sea eagle's video-call that
causes her to freeze,
ease back on the throttle

and research, in the lilting soar
of its silver-white wings,
this binary of tranquillity
and flash-dive luminance.

Every olive counts
New Harbour, Tasmania

The wind flings my flatbread off my lap,
two olives land in the sand.
I am instructed to pick them up, wash them off.

The departing tide arranges
thousands of translucent blue bodies
and long, opaque tails on the sand.
A bluebottle invasion
shrivelling in the sun.

We skinny-dip in the creek's
thwarted mouth.
Breaststroke around in the metre-deep fresh water
backed up behind the beach.
The top two centimetres, warmed by the sun.
Below that
very refreshing.
Paddle around, goose-bumped,
gazing at seagulls, eucalypts, clouds.
Drying off, we anticipate
a slightly less smelly night in the tent.

I am chastised
for snacking on lunch crackers
before bed.

This is the wild South-West.
Skies menace grey clouds,
cold wind whips into our bones
as we sit on the ground, puffed up
in down jackets, fleece beanies,
long pants and thick socks,
wondering where summer's gone.

**Advice for those who find themselves doing long bushwalks
for some crazy reason they can't remember**

When walking is trudging,
when you're simply soldiering onwards,
it pays to think of nothing,
to morph into a zombie
of automated movement,
each foot seeking a steady step
of its own accord.

You are the body being hauled along
by two fully capable legs
so chill out, think of nothing.

Don't think of how refugees
would feel fleeing Iraq
with everything they could haul along
on mine-pocked, death-rocked roads.

Don't dwell on how it would feel
to be an Aboriginal girl
following a rabbit proof fence
through the desert
or to be a soldier
slogging through mud on Kokoda's trail…
these thoughts will leave you
more weary.

And don't try thinking that your pack
is as light as a feather —
your mind is not stupid and will
overcompensate to prove you wrong.

Don't pretend your destination is just

                            rise
                 next
      that
beyond

as your legs will go on strike
when you arrive to find

               rise.
        another
just

Don't count your steps as that will
amplify your challenge and disturb you.

Don't think of poems
to describe the scenery
as your eyes will soften
so you trip.

No, best to think of nothing,
let your legs carry you along,
relax into the monotonous aching
of this ancient activity.

Definitely don't think about
fish and chips
or the cushy sofa at home.

Whitewater Wall

time alone
legs sun-balmed

granite boulders slow my pulse
give my hands something to trust

stressors slip through cracks
meld into pounding ocean below

in the distance
black-skinned and rubbery

you're a standing piece of kelp
cold and dripping, holding abalone

our friend is a red speck
clinging to peach-coloured cliff

bits of gear clink on waist
each finger-muscle strains to grip rock

harnessed below, another friend
coaxes rope

thoughts form and morph
into the grand landscape of clouds

sun sinks
to the other side of the world

scramble back to base
settle on logs

pass around beer, salty chips
shush away persistent possums

the cold herds us into tents
silk liners, fluffy bags

tired muscled arms
warm embrace

Morning meteorology

The paper struggles out of its plastic wrap,
uncurls to declare —
Johannesburg — haze,
Mexico City — smoke.
Stockholm — fresh,
Rome knows mist.

Here in Hobart —
        sun, 8-17°C.

Isobars separate themselves politely.
A high drifts by.

My orange juice and I study
the UV Index (moderate),
the week's outlook,
the moon's cycles.

I see some black-and-white sea breezes,
swell three-point-five metres,
note the wind angling from the west.
Disregard the tides — tedious for boatless people.

To see the world's weather in a crunch of cornflakes,
have it lying open on the table,
is to feel connected, I guess.

Soon I will venture out,
feel the draught against my cheek,
wonder where it has been —

whose breath I am inhaling.

High-density foam gets me through

It's a cheapo.
Purple, thin, high density-foam
kid-scribbled (yellow fluoro) in one corner.
Smells artificial.
No idea when I got it
or from where.

Rolling out my yoga mat cues
me-time,
conscious, deeper
slower breaths,
containment.

I lay it flat
in my extra-wide hallway,
door closed against lounge-room squabbles.

When I step on it
I release.

When I lie on it
I sink.

The soft hand of gravity
cradles me,
the floor pledges loyal support.

Downward dog inversions
entice my mind
to suspend worry
and planning.

I stay —
moving chest down, butt raised —
stern shoulder blades   separating.

Lunges usher my centre down
direct me
              away from rumination
invite me
home to my body
to notice
its movements
its breathing.

Child's pose is my harbour
forward-fold my retreat.

Warriors fortify.
Standing wide-legged
knees bent
arms out, pointing —
core clenches
muscles steady
strength builds.

Balance postures offer
just-right challenges.
My favourite: the one-legged tree
with eyes focused on a
point   in front
palms together, raised skywards.

I can cope with this one-legged tree.
For this time
on this thin, grippy mat
I can cope.

Ready for more than nursery rhymes

Poetry,
I've kept my distance from you for three-and-a-half years
and that's ok
because I was making new people —
two of them —
and really, life trumps poetry.

But without poetry,
life is a bleached coral reef,
missing connections, colour and zest,
so I am edging back to you
in between nappy changes and lullabies,
liquid Panadol and my own lonely pillow.

Poetry,
forgive me for snubbing you.
Remind me how to observe
more than the swollen gums of the next tooth,
more than the yearning for sleep-ins.
Come and save me
from the repetition of the weekly vacuum,
the dreaded bath-scrub, the urgent late-afternoon question
        of what to cook.

I know some things, like these indescribable
love-blossomed smiles from my babies
are outside your scope of practice,
but I need you to rescue me from burnt meatballs,
temper tantrums at the kitchen gate
and this chasm between experience
        and words.

Poetry, I've taken advantage of your patience.
        Will you have me back?

When I touch your nose you smile

You're perfectly formed –

your pulsating fontanelle,
intricate ears,
downy hair.
The capillary calligraphy of your eyelids,
plump hand
separated from your arm by an origami crease.

Your little sneezes –
quick, sweet concise.
Mine are loud, large,
        jolting you off my breast.

You coo at me,
        I coo at you.
Your excitement bursts through flapping arms,
                wriggling torso, kicking legs;
a horizontal happy dance.
Hey Diddle Diddle evokes a throaty one-pitched laugh;
any song captures you, wide-eyed.

On your back, legs up, sucking your toes,
you are my roly-poly.
When your father lifts you naked and wet from the bath,
I remember glimpsing you above the khaki screen
        as they lifted you from me,
        vigorous and complete,
how relieved,
how ecstatic I was
to meet you.

Shining eyes and trilling squeals define delight.
When you cry, your bottom lip drops and quivers,
mouth squares,
from jubilant to heartbroken in a second.

You roll onto your tummy,
glance around to see who's there to warble praise,
break into a proud grin,
sustain adept locust and cobra poses,
do push-ups
before you rest, head to one side,
sucking the two middle fingers of your left hand.

When the world is new

At ten months — toys are passé.
Instead there is a tight grip on keys and wallets,
an urge to suck handbag straps,
master zips,
swipe the screen on my phone.
Able to stand on toes and peer over the edge of the table,
pudgy fingers find sunglasses and papers to pull.

The weekend dresses the mountain in snow.
We layer up, though she whips off her beanie
and peels open the velcro on her shoes.
Captivated by kids who can walk and run,
she commando-crawls after them.
Glares at people who talk to her,
waves after they've turned away.

I mix tahini with her rice cereal, tuna with pureed veg,
watch her respond to the sultana packet
with arm-flapping glee.
She slips peas into her mouth like lollies,
hoiks annoying citrus onto the floor,
gives me a surprised 'ooh' that could be feigned,
leans over her tray to study the mess.

She lifts my top and squeals at my squishy belly, her old home.
(She wouldn't get her bond back).
If I put music on, she turbo-crawls to the stereo shelf,
stands close, mosh-style, bopping to the beat.

We mimic each other's vocalisations.
She ramps it up to high-pitched shrills — and wins.
Peek-a-boo, tug-of-war, upside down,
row-row-your-boat — so many reasons to ignore the housework.

I sit her down on a beach and laugh
as her arms spring up in surprise, oohing and aahing at the ocean.
She stares at it, turns questioningly to me,

back at it, back at me, wanting me to explain this wondrous, fluid mass
that spills foam onto the sand while thundering softly.
The sand is objectionable – she touches it just enough to know.
It sticks to the fingers she sucks – screws up her face, keeps sucking.

This winter is like no other winter:
its gloom has been rumbled and dismissed
by this exclaiming baby
who would put the whole world into her mouth.

The purposeful occupations of a two-year-old

wall scribbling
    sand throwing

toast tossing
    crumb swiping

clothes snipping
    backyard absconding

necklace snapping
    toy scattering

baby-wipe extracting
    carpet weeing

keyboard pressing
    CD scattering

sunglasses stretching
    pencil case upending

shelf decluttering
    cutlery clanging

sister's hair yanking
    arm biting

towel evading
    hairbrush dodging

first story competing
    in-to-bed protesting

stick poking
    rash cream smearing

cup tipping
    chewed cashew spitting

bead sucking
    roadside dashing

crayon cracking
    vacuum-cleaner stopping

tissue-box emptying
    nappy-change resisting

phone tampering
    stereo cords unplugging

nail scissors pilfering
    couch trampolining

book ripping
    roast dinner refusing

leg pinching
    open fridge loitering

nude skedaddling
    gorilla *jamas* demanding

lap wrestling
    middle-of-the-night calling

The bars of the cot don't just trap the baby

I am locked beside them

uselessly patting the swaddled, blanketed lump

screaming inside my skull for him

to stop his nerve-crushing ululations

his ridiculous struggle against sleep

my back aches like it's already morning

like it's already my eighth decade

a future incarcerated

by this eternal now

O sugar

Added fructose fast-tracks it to the liver,
transforms into fat.
The limit — six teaspoons a day.
Lamington fingers — one-and-a-half teaspoons each!
My budget blown eating three
with my tea.

All the cornflake biscuits,
date kisses,
chocolate slices
and cupcakes we devoured
after school growing up,
all the virtuous baking I planned to do
for my kids,
using recipes handed down two generations,
no longer virtuous at all!

O sugar,
I learn your ways, build my strength,
divorce you.
But at work there are cakes I can't resist,
mid-afternoon chocolate cravings.
I discover home-baked sugar-free cakes made for little mouths
are hard for anyone to swallow.
I take you back.

When breastfeeding in the middle of the night,
Monte Carlos and Mars Bars
reach out and offer sweet support.

In the early afternoons when kids won't succumb to naps
I stare accusingly at the clocks —
surely they're broken, it can't just be 1pm!
You reach out your white, brown or syrupy arms,
attend to my exhaustion
in ways that no-one else will.

Later I read blogs and watch docos
on the health crisis caused by sugar
hidden in processed foods.
I march away again.

But it doesn't take much — a few nights with a sick baby,
an afternoon of sibling whinging and snatching,
dirty clothes looming like Mount Everest in the laundry —
you sweet-talk your way back through the door.

Sultanas, biscuits and
chocolate-cherry slices seduce —
you hook me with your familiar buzz.

O sugar, you give me that shot of energy
to handle the next domestic catastrophe —
an upended pot plant,
custard clotting and burning as I respond to a tricycle stack.

When will I muster the strength
to turn to wholefoods,
long-lasting, slow-release foods,
learn to turn my back on you, again?

Still has the touch

for Anne Joan Austin, Great-grandmother

Been entertaining next door neighbour's flies,
she grins at me across the table set
with lamingtons, shop-bought — against her pride.
They'll have to do, can't bake much now, my pet.
Remember when I used to let you wrap
lettuce leaves with sugar — my little treat —
and you'd do anything to avoid your daily nap
so we'd go for walks all up and down the street.

Baby frets —   despite an arthritic spine
she maneuvers down next to him on the floor.
It's been a long time since I had all mine,
I don't know how to soothe them anymore.
Yet her wrinkled touch slows his restless cries
or did he catch the incandescence in her eyes?

The lap portal

They love me reading to them.

Both still small enough to sit on my lap,
legs either side of each of mine.

First I read a chapter of her fairy story
then his dinosaur picture book.
He loves the library's "Rex wrecks it" —
can relate to Rex
who can't resist the urge to scuttle towers, sandcastles.

There are over a hundred Rainbow Magic fairy stories
and she never loses interest
in their predictable adventures.

Sometimes I wish I had all day to read to them
but there is always so much to do —
no-one else to do it.

She is on the cusp of learning to read.
Will I wish, in a few short years,
that I left the clothes unfolded,
served tinned spaghetti on toast,
made more time for sitting
with my arms around them
venturing into magical worlds together?

Gorilla pyjamas

Second-hand, they were already pretty shabby
but night after night he requested *grilla jamas,*
beamed when we put them on over his nappy
and now-not-so-white bodysuit.

After washing he'd grab them off the indoor clothes rack,
declaring they were dry though they could be soaking.
I'd chase him round the house to grab them back,
hang them on the highest rung.

Once he got ready for playgroup himself,
disappearing into his bedroom to pull them on,
adding ugg-boots and sunnies,
emerging proud as punch.

When bigger, he worked on honing his skills with the buttons.
I think he got two years out of them
before the flannelette wore through at the knees,
his limbs grew too far from the hems.

After a few days of warning and explaining,
I tossed them in the kitchen bin.
He kept asking for them for days,
then switched to requesting

I put them on the shopping list,
buy him new ones.
I tried my best, but gorilla jamas are not easy to find.
His first real lesson in loss.

Sonnet for lost lasts

His class lines up in pairs at the berry farm.
His free hand is held out for me to find.
I'm surprised to feel his whole hand in my palm:
he used to curl his fingers round one of mine.
Another little last, like the daytime nap?
Last time I hold his hand to cross a street,
last picture book read snuggled in my lap,
the final time I help him brush his teeth.
When will be the last we share a bath?
No camera will snap the final trolley ride,
the moment plastic cups give way to glass.
His fluffy monkey comforter will slide —
with the glee he gets from using arms to fart —
into that chest of lost lasts in my heart.

No magic wand

Can you read us a book or play a game with us, Mum?
I'm folding clothes and collecting things off the floor –
I'll play with you after all the chores are done.

I'm cleaning the kitchen and wiping up all the crumbs.
But what can we do Mum? You know, we're just so bored!
Can you read a book or play a game with us, Mum?

No, I'm paying bills and look there's more than one.
I'm putting this washing on and hanging out more,
I can play with you after all the chores are done.

Mum! He's not playing properly! He's saying he's won!
Mum! He's messing up all the cards and games in the drawer!
Can you please read a book or play a game with us, Mum?

Watching you wash the dishes and vacuum isn't fun!
Can we do some craft together or go for a walk?
I said I can play after all the chores are done.

Lunches won't make themselves, though that'd be fun.
A wand would come in handy, that's for sure.
Can you read a book now or play a game with us, Mum?
All right, I'll play for a bit, these chores won't ever be done.

Outing

I did not foresee
how life could contract

so that
walking   the pram   to the park

is the pinnacle

of my week

my only
spontaneous
adventure

Urgencies

the rain thrums on our heads as we
swarm with all the others to shelter

you request – I hoist you up,
comb your wet hair with my fingers

we wait out the downpour,
or we would have,

if you didn't shout:
I need to go to the toilet, now!

Salmon ponds

gorgeous sibling Facebook photos
matching navy track pants,
one with pink beanie and pom-pom on top, one with white wispy hair
arm around the other's shoulders, looking at the camera, smiling cutely

it was freezing
my hands turned to ice in ten minutes
it was day eight of husband being away for work
it was an outing planned for the sanity-salvaging forty-five minute drive
        there and back
it was the morning after being up through the night with toddler teething
        troubles,
woken early by daughter with phantom wet undies
it was after toy-pram fights and three time-outs before packing the bag

on the way there, after wrestling son into seat with some force,
after stopping numerous times to cajole him to put arms back in straps,
after he removed shoes and socks which had been a struggle to put on,
after he ripped a page out of my favourite childhood book,
it was pointing out cows and swans,
explaining paper mills and singing along as the frog jumped out of the pond

on the way home it was relieved silence as they both slept and I wondered
how to resuscitate my mood, where to suture my patience,
how a simple outing could have been so onerous

it was only the small things,
the fights over fish feed,
pellets flung to the ground as one snatched a cup from the other,
the anxiety of watching a toddler saunter close to the edge
the slow-motion response to my *Look! A fish jumped!*
Look! A fish swimming, see its colourful tail swishing!
my pointing and exclaiming
which failed to assist them to ever spot the fish

the fact that neither ate their treat — maple syrup pancakes —
so I ate them all and felt sick and bulky,
that son started pulling apart the already-ripped back of his highchair
and wouldn't desist,
that he cried out repeatedly to be let down when I was still sipping my tea,
that they took turns banging their spoons on the table,
the trip to the loo with me wrestling him away from bin, toilet paper,
        tap, soap,
grabbing him up as he commando-crawled across the dirty floor to evade me,
the second trip to the loo thirty minutes later which resulted in no
        more three-year-old wee
just more two-year-old wrestling

the fights over sandwiches, drink bottles
the leisurely walk along the creek where I was hoping
to stretch my legs, get a slight pace going to warm up,
but where I had to stop every metre
because son refused to sit in pram,
wouldn't walk in the right direction
or actually follow any instructions to leave the gate open /
don't climb through the creek fence / hurry up
and daughter refused to hop out when I did finally convince son to hop in

it's just little things, over-reactions,
inflated expectations, taking things too seriously,
but look, here are my adorable children
smiling sweetly at the camera, her arm around his shoulders
beside the glistening pond —
imagine if you will, the lovely time we had

Quality time

my iPhone —
    Facebook
    weather
    calendar
    emails
    texts
    news
my curved back
my slight frown

my two-year old —
    shaking her red egg-shaped maraca
    beaming at me
    until I notice
    her joy

Ode to a park bench

Thanks
for taking me,
the weight of me,
the hard, the soft, the heft, the ache of me,
for being still,
for being
here,
where I can stop, sit
push my feet down onto these paving stones
rein in shaky wayward breaths,
counting back from ten.

Thoughts weft and jostle.
I imagine them passing by
like cars
like clouds
but one doesn't drift,
it lodges its pungent bulk next to me,
You are a bad mum, it snarls.
My guts sink into these soles, these stones.

You listen too,
your weather-hardened boards frown.
You hold me.
Your planks curve against my bumpy spine,
buttress my weary back.

I tune in to the quietly ecstatic trees,
rustling maroon leaves,
lingering taste of soy chai tea,
smell of mulch,
the salty tang of the neighbouring, impervious sea.

Soon the thought gets bored
and moves along.
I study your russet grainy wood,
lean my right side against your steel armrest,
feel the tree-born goodness of you
under my thighs.

You furnish me with the strength to rise.

Self-portrait in 114 words

I slouch. When I stand tall I feel too tall. If I see someone's bent
shoulders and humped back, I jerk upright. But most of the time
I'm too busy to be aware of my upper torso scrunching towards the
floor. I focus on my never-ending tasks. Work, kids, husband, shops,
dishes, dinner, washing, events. I think of ways to hide sweet potato in
macaroni cheese and kidney beans in chocolate cake. I prioritise sleep.
Once I led a group who tried to change the world. We met, taught,
wrote, rallied. Now I try to stop the world burning in my spare time.
One day I hope I'll stand tall without thinking about it.

No razors for me

I must have been encircled by green and purple ribbons
much younger than I thought,
because I made my stand at age fourteen,
when school-crafted conformity
failed to grip me completely.

It's hard to keep hairy legs hidden through a Queensland summer
and by then mine were hairier than most.
I thought of how God's designs were so exact, (raised a Catholic)
and how unfair it was that boys never had to think twice
about a razor for their legs.

I refused to dabble in the different forms of hair removal
discussed during recess and lunch;
I refused to remove any of it.

The girls could see my point – the beauty myth and all that –
but my defiance slipped off them smoothly.
The boys teased, of course – mostly behind my back –
but just often enough to my face to know that they called me
Kiwifruit Legs.

I won some respect when I stood up to the teacher
in defence of one boy's messy hairdo –
must have been on a *we can all do what we like with our own hair* crusade.

I gave in for my school formal –
couldn't accessorise a puffy satin dress with carpet-covered calves –
the senior school style-police won the battle.

It's been years since I've scraped a razor along my shins.
Since then I've moved on from hair rights
to human rights.

Smartphone confessions

I look at my phone while the kids cling to my legs and ask for Weetbix,
check that no-one called, texted, messaged or emailed me through the night,
turn it from silent to sound, plug it in to charge.
I look at my phone after rinsing cereal bowls,
to check the weather and the UV index on the bureau's website,
today's events on the calendar.
I brush all our teeth, hair, then look at my phone to add currants,
toothpaste and toilet paper to the shopping list.
I look at my phone to add things to the to-do list as they come to mind –
post back after-school-care forms, pay Telstra bill.

The kids are playing with dolls and prams so I look at my phone to check
        Facebook
to see who is doing what, where and with whom,
to glance at the news headlines, add some article links
to my never-ending list of saves.
I look at my phone to text a friend about a movie night, RSVP to a kid's party.
I look at my phone to research the best price and where to buy kids' goggles.
I look at my phone to take photos,
film the kids dancing around the lounge in ladybird costumes.

I look at my phone to find the recipe for tonight's couscous and meatball dinner,
the opening hours of Kindergym.
I look at my phone to message someone about buying their second-hand pram,
then in the car I look at my phone for directions to their house.
I look at my phone to check the TV guide for Play School times,
to research the appropriate age to watch the movie, Trolls.

I look at my phone as my daughter describes her doll's fifth birthday party,
to reschedule the dentist
and add to the list of things to note in the kids' diary this month.
I look at my phone to add another book to my Goodreads list,
rate the one I've just read,
check my emails again,
wish a friend Happy Birthday on Facebook,
and click "I'm Going" to the Teddy Bears Picnic.

While the kids wriggle in their booster chairs and drop muffin crumbs on
          the floor
I look at my phone to check that our dream house hasn't appeared on
          realestate.com.

When I look at my phone
all my kids see
is their mother, looking at her phone.
My four-year-old sometimes brings it to me as I wake up – *Here's your phone,
          Mummy.*
When she was two, she asked me if we could go to the shops
to buy her one.

The morning trench

Each bowl of milk-drenched Weetbix revolves
in the yellow-lit microwave for forty seconds.
Four little hands push, shoulders clash
as they grapple over the Peter Rabbit cup.

After I assign currants, water, spoons and bib,
push in, strap in, bums on seats,
my muesli is camouflage against the table.
I scoop it in like gruel.

A stinky-nappy stoush, sock-and-shoe skirmish,
hair-brush hustle, toothpaste affray,
the usual provisioning of the pack
delay our advance into this gelid day.
The path lurks narrow and frangible.

Once I was ebullient about a walk in the park —
chuckles on swings were tangible,
slides would see faces brighten,
but today, as one rips the cover off Fox in Socks
and the other liberates arms from harness,
my tired eyebrows tighten.

The space inside my fists

after an infinite day
after an hour cooking
        fetching
        serving
(non)reacting to food-rejections
high-pitched operatic demands from the three-year-old
        for pink cup not Sesame Street one
        spoon not fork

after I sit down, take two mouthfuls
        after my two-year old spits half-masticated tortellini on floor
        upends bowl of stir-fry over tray

I launch up, snavel it back into bowl
        explode – *When will I ever get to eat my friggin' dinner in peace!*
stomp into kitchen, grab rag, wipe floor, flick into sink
        collapse into chair,
        eat in a dumping wave of agitation

today I see that even half-an-hour away
        washes back tenderness
a long-anticipated walk on a beach in the sun's envelope
        restores patience

without meaning to, I collect shells for them,
conical sand-snails, king scallops, solid air-breathers, venus clams,
step-by-sand-softened-step I think of the craft we could do with them,
        hope they cherish their beauty
        when I open my fists and offer them

then I catch myself

gum trees tall dark silhouettes against the dusk-dreaming sky
ocean soft symphony scent of wood-smoke shacks
flat, numbered avenues wending behind rock-crested coast

a few moments of phone-free anxiety – what if I get lost don't have Google Maps
what if it gets dark don't have my phone torch
what if I need to call someone

then I catch myself
relax
enjoy the beauty of walking at dusk
birdcalls
the novelty of pre-dinner exercise

recall strolls round the block with mum in my hometown holding hands

catch glimpses of other people's early evening routines their couches TV shows
before curtains slide against steadily advancing night

relish this escape
striding freely through crisp air

Tonight, soup

the last four years and five months she has prepared food for her children
introduced one taste at a time in puree form
vigilant for allergic reactions
served soft finger foods in small portions
nervous about choking
(the second child gagged and vomited on-and-off for months)
dealt with all sorts of food refusals
wielded armfuls of kid-friendly, healthy recipes, mostly in vain
ploughed through dietician-recommended advice books
followed the *division of responsibility* as best she could
even started eating some meat for the first time in twenty years
as sometimes it was the only practical way to feed herself

lentil and vegetable soup
nothing fancy, but she knows
her husband won't eat it
as lentils don't agree with him
her kids won't eat it
as they won't permit pulses, vegetables or soup
anywhere near their mouths
but for once she doesn't care
onions, garlic, carrots, cauliflower, lentils
vegetable stock, salt, pepper, cumin

her husband is home, floundering to devise dinner for the kids
she relents, fetches him frozen meatballs, tin of spaghetti
but focuses back on her soup

the day is cold and she craves the warmth of it
she's been fighting a sore throat
and she hungers for the health of it
easy to prepare, no recipe required
when it's ready she sits down with her ceramic,
non-dishwasher-safe, hand-painted bowl, steaming
everything can wait until she's eaten her soup

Empty house alien

There is space
around me,
in me.

I circle through the lounge,
the kitchen
the bedroom,
lost in orbit.

This year they've reached
the miraculous ages of five and seven –
both in full-time school.
Today they sped off, smiling.

My gaze lands
on the kettle,
the couch,
the kitchen table –
all strangely foreign.

I try to write
but it's as if my brain resolves
to think in French
and I've forgotten all the words
except
Merci.

New day of freedom

What did I do on my first day off
when my youngest started school?

Sat on my bed and read love poems,
ordered toilet paper through a neighbourhood bulk-buy,
ate nectarine on toast — mindfully, that is —
noticing texture, crunch, taste, my usual urge for haste.

I set up my computer, made a new file —
    Poetry 2021

and typed this,
doing my best to tune out my husband's video-call work meetings
and the little specks of guilt
settling with dust
over the floorboards.

Serve it up

Malted rye toast
a flicker of olive oil
thinly sliced plums on top.

Tea,
solitude,
plush patch of grass.

Sandals off,
notebook ready,
wrists relaxed.

Patience —

words will come
like ants to crumbs.

Sharks circle

Notifications lodge in my inbox like clots:
          another case in class;
          two in after-school care.

I work doubly hard
covering for a colleague in iso with her kids
          who then catches it too.

My daughter reports
her best friend wasn't at school today.
          She has Covid.

Did you sit next to her yesterday?
          All day.
Play with her?
          Of course, recess and lunch.

I stock up on groceries,
psych myself up, warn my boss.
          The sharks are circling, she jokes.

And then it's here.

My daughter, normally
speeding to the table for dinner,
          doesn't want any.
Flounders on the couch with headaches,
          a fever.

Two years into the pandemic,
three months after open borders,
it's our turn.

Attack of the killer swab

Rapid Antigen Tests should be easy,
especially twinned with lollipops.
We tout them as home science experiments
to get outcomes we're all vitally interested in,

but swiping the swab five times around
each kid-sized nostril
is attempted murder.
       Heads jerk back in horror
each time the small white stick looms close –
there's gagging and shouting and resisting
til both swabber and swabee spurt fury.

After the act is done
we place the test cassette on the bench,
set the kitchen timer for fifteen minutes
and will it to show a line – even a faint one –
next to the T

so we don't have to do it all again tomorrow,
so we can start the real timer –
the seven day iso one –
face the enemy head-on.

But it's not positive.

I'm up through the night administering Panadol
and the next morning I drive her to get a PCR,
thinking a professional might be more able
to collect nasal mucous with ease.

Instead it's a hostage scene —
for twenty minutes
a stubborn, terrified eight-year-old holds up
two nurses and a security guard,
all trying their best to convince her to put down the hands
frantically shielding her nose and mouth.

Cars back up behind us,
the guard brandishes a Frozen movie Elsa certificate
with my daughter's name on it in pink curly capitals,
I pledge lollies and TV all day
and just when I'm about to sacrifice
the knowing —
to accept defeat —
she reluctantly consents
to just the nose part of the test.

Later that day we get the text —
positive.

Plague house

We've been warned about this threat for more than two years.
It's dominated newsfeeds, papers,
radio and TV,
conversations in every context.

This semi-apocalypse we've been warding off with
masks, sanitiser
and ever-changing rules
has now breached our defences,
is here in this house.

It feels strange, momentous.
I'm in suspense all week
wondering if and when I'll get it.

It might be sensible
but I won't mask up
against you, my child.
You already complain about feeling unloved
and diseased
when we recoil at your cough,
cry for you not to breathe in our faces.

I will not socially distance from you.
I dispense cuddles, Panadol,
join you at the table for dinner,
read stories with you on the couch
and brush your hair and teeth
like normal.

But I didn't mean to kiss you on the forehead
as I tucked you into bed.

Tainted gifts

Our little veggie garden is flashing red,
flourishing with San Marzano, Grosse Lisse,
Tiny Tim and Tommy Toes.
I pluck bowlfuls from the bushes.
Glossy balls of flavour surrender to my fingers
but no-one has much appetite —
they amass in the fridge.

I offer some to my neighbour over the fence and she's keen
but five minutes later,
after I've filled a container of mixed variety
and stand four metres in front of her,
ready to place my offering on the ground,
her face flickers concern, second thoughts.
I pause, embarrassed at my tainted gifts.
We decide it's not safe for her to accept,
not knowing how to properly sanitise tomatoes.

Mask up

Mask up
the Covid bogeyman hasn't yet found the exit —
uninvited guest at a party
telling too many tedious tales
get intimate with your own expired air
the garlic memory of your lunchtime focaccia
the quickening heat of your unsettled breaths

Mask up
it's a new way of life
maintaining life is the purpose
although it seems like all they do is interrupt
the facial expressions and connections that enrich
don't turn to touch to compensate
or we'll all have to sanitise again

Mask up
it's the new fashion
choose your mask to match your outfit
and don't forget which one is clean
which was yesterday's that needs a wash
is there any point to make-up
or toothpicks anymore?

Mask up
even if it scares the kids
feels like we're in a new apocalypse
these cloth and paper defences
promise to keep your germs out
and my germs in
let's share other things instead
like hopes and fears
and all the fragile hesitations in between

Monitoring devices

My son succumbs on official Day Two.
This is when the real fun begins, I grimace,
thinking of the croup that descends with any ordinary cold
and spars with him for breath at 3am,
skinny ribcage fighting hard.
How much worse will it be with Covid?

I call the Covid-at-Home team
three times
and just before dinner someone with qualifications
calls back.
Sitting on my bed at night,
worrying instead of reading,
I hear a delivery van pull up,
drop a box at the door.
I inspect the forehead thermometer,
pulse oximeter and smart phone,
muster energy to read pages of instructions
and my shoulders release,
knowing I'll be able to measure oxygen levels
if he's gripped by an attack through the night.
I feel equipped,
grateful for devices, a 1800 number
and public health support.

We work out we have to clamp the oximeter over his thumb,
his other fingers too small to register.
We submit readings daily after 11am —
the phone reminds us and reminds us
until we do as it says.

He slept well except …

I sleep in the spare bed in my son's room
because when he gets sick he gets scared
and I can stay alert to his breathing.

One morning when we wake I ask him how he slept —

Good, but you did scare me when you oinked.

What do you mean, I oinked?

He demonstrates a single snuffly snore
and I laugh on and off all day about *oinking.*

Breathing

I arm my son with croup medication

and the croup doesn't strike.

As each night passes
I breathe easier.

Iso exhaustion

I collapse into bed, wondering if my headache
is the beginnings of Covid

or anxiety-and-kid-disrupted sleep,

or just the exhaustion
of managing fighting siblings
not at their best?

Easter egg hunt

While they're busy with home-school and Minecraft
I hide eggs in the backyard –
an early Easter treat to brighten lockdown.
The sun joins in, melting some by the time
my daughter's lesson finishes
and I let them loose.

My son gives up after finding just two –
lethargy conquering his usual persistence.
With encouragement he finds one in the barbecue
and squeezes it to prove how much it's melted.
Chocolate squirts onto the floorboards
making another mess for me to clean.

A toy chick gets covered
by a second oozing egg
and doesn't withstand its wash –
its bedraggled fluff and half-mangled head
become my Covid mascot.

My son unwraps a medium-sized egg,
takes a bite – *yuck!*,
abandons it on the bench.
He must be sick.

Outsiders

Everyone offers to deliver groceries.
But we don't need groceries.
Food is going bad in the fridge
because no-one wants to eat.

My husband returns from Flinders Island,
drops bread and milk at the door.
He stands three metres away, mask on, to talk.
My son runs to hug him.
We shout in unison —
No!

Last one standing

A sore throat on Day Six fells burgeoning thoughts
about harbouring a strong constitution.

I almost enjoy doing a RAT on myself —
it's a breeze compared to doing it on the kids.

A sore throat and fuzzy head weighs me down the next day
before another RAT comes clean with the truth.

At least the seven-day stay-at-home rule
and the desire to protect others from the plague
means there's no guilt involved
in taking leave from work.

Oriental lilies

These magnificent flowers —
two bunches —
are my husband's and sister-in-law's
ways of acknowledging my ordeal
and showing me they care.
In this lonely home
they open slowly.

Dramatic hot pink tepals, fringed by white,
liberate six pollen-clad stamens
to stand guard around
striking purple stigmas.
During Day Thirteen,
when my yearnings for bushwalks and cafes peak,
they blast their fragrance into the rooms
where I am trapped.

At least I can tell that Covid
hasn't plundered my olfactory sense
but this inebriating odour
is the scent of my arrest.

My first Uber Eats

Vegan chicken pizza.

What a treat
to have an appetite again
and, with a few taps on my phone,
people to cater to it.

Retail therapy

Once I'm well
and out,
I splurge on new cushions for the lounge,
colour-matching with the sales assistant
mask-free.

I'm invincible,
immune,
liberated.

JobSeeker in the time of Coronavirus

She waters the weeds in the alleyway,
hoping they will flower.
Evenings she pads slowly past the street's high fences,
wishing she could enjoy the gardens they seclude.

She kisses the letter that tells her about the Coronavirus Supplement,
spends her first payment on grocery basics, used timber
to build a patio planter box,
herbs she introduces to the soil.

Returns to the nursery the next day,
dodging boys barrelling along the footpath on scooters,
staggers home, legs and arms complaining,
with a dwarf pomegranate tree in a large green ceramic pot.

Squats to position it to the left of her paint-blistered front door.
Its future fruit — shiny red and hard,
        hiding hundreds of sweet juicy gems
        to roll and explode in her mouth —

something now
            to look forward to.

Catch: a break

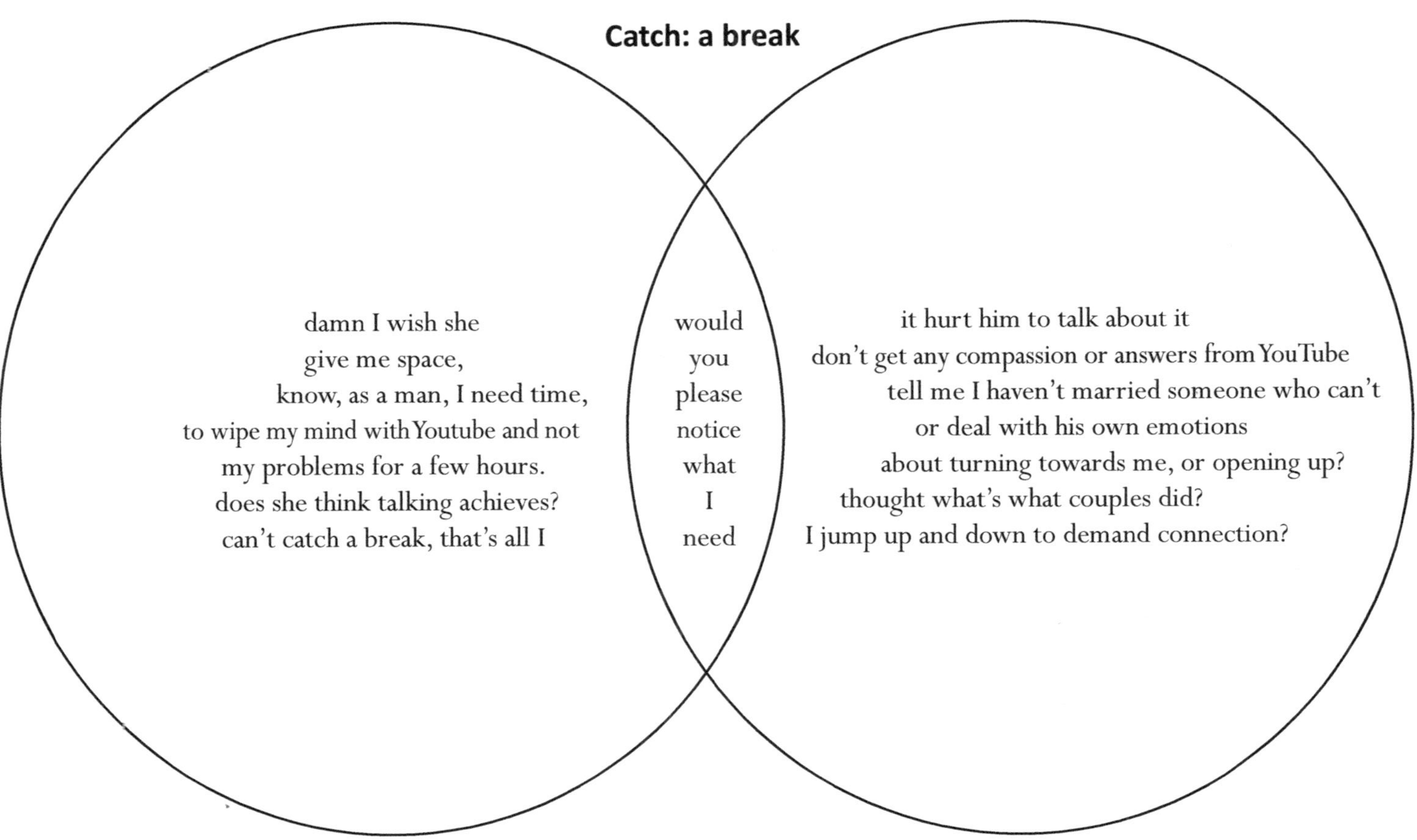

Fault lines

we spit molten opinions at each other
between morning tea and lunch
wonder how the day erupted

lava flows
between lunch and dinner
sulking   each with our own screens

avoiding   in our rooms
thick breaths flow
anger solidifies

after the kitchen's clean and the kids are dreaming
we exchange bills
you pay Telstra,   I'll pay Aurora

in the fertile volcanic soil
we sew tentative seeds of repair
with BPAY numbers

The failure of the favourite song

Intimacy
is the poncho worn
over shivering shoulders,
hands cold.

It was okay before but now
it's intolerable —
this sweet tooth-decaying affection.

Our conversations
run as parallel as
the lines we drive beside,
intimating crossroads ahead,
a stop sign.

The terminal velocity of raindrops

"The impact force of the raindrop is dependent on the terminal velocity of the raindrop, which is a function of diameter." — Perera et al.

we avoid eye   any   contact
the diameter of animosity widens,
surfaces tighten

we hint at needs via intermittent drizzle —
easy to ignore,
useless at quenching thirst

I wait for him   to organise a date·
cook dinner
signal he wants to spend time

serious clouds accumulate
wind shrieks
rain smashes windows

I salute the sun on my mat in the lounge
hands ply skywards
face panoramic views of grey

tonight I meet a girlfriend at a wine bar
he eats chips and watches violence on Netflix

Drapery

The sixth curtain sprawls on a chair.
I can't iron any more.
The gap can stay.
I don't mind seeing the small fairy lights of town.

Finally, after a day's acting at work,
the dinner table, the kitchen bench,
both of us talking to the kids
but not each other,

I keel into bed,
grip the doona and grieve
for the crinkled curtain,
the gap

    all that was whole between us.

Signal strength

At the end of a long day
comfort materialises before me —
couch, cushion, cup of rooibos tea.

News stories of more assaults beam
into my Facebook feed.
I place my phone face-down on the table
next to the precarious tower of kids' books.

I ponder bed, wonder if nightmares
will abduct me tonight,
return me with racing heart, sweat-stuck
to cloistering sheets.

I meet your gaze as you look up
from YouTubing on the iPad,
a question floats across.

Instead of communicating about the dishwasher
(why won't the bulk-buy powder dispense during a cycle?)
or ignoring each other, lured into
the sticky world-wide-web,
we study the other's expression,
detect a yearning for affection.

You remove headphones,
put down the iPad, move closer.

Time to test
and upgrade
our connection.

Acknowledgements

Grateful acknowledgment is made to the editors of the following journals where many of these poems first appeared (sometimes in earlier versions): *JobSeeker in the time of Coronavirus* and *First day falling* were published in Burrow; *The failure of the favourite song* was published in Prospect; *Sonnet for lost lasts* in the Communion Arts Journal; *Advice for those who find themselves doing long bushwalks for some crazy reason they can't remember* in Poetry Matters Democratic Republic; *Mask up* in Poetry in the Hospital; *Serve it up* was included in WordXimage's Andrew Bennett Ekphrastic Poems and *Dust* was published as part of The Brew project.

Outing was published in Poems From The Dig Anthology; *When the world is new, The purposeful occupations of a two-year-old* and *Smartphone confessions* were published in When the world is new – Fellowship of Australian Writers (FAW) Tasmanian Anthology and *Ready for more than nursery rhymes* is the opening poem in the 2022 anthology Quicksilver Water: Oasis Women Poets. *Every olive counts* was published in The World According to Us, 2023 Anthology FAW Northwest Writers Tasmania.

A different kind of online won the 2023 FAW Tasmanian Poetry Prize. *Whitewater Wall* was commended in the FAW Norma and Colin Knight Poetry Award 2009, *then I catch myself* was awarded a Special Mention in 2021 and *The ring shoots sparkles* and *Ode to a park bench* were commended in the same award in 2022.

The term *lost lasts* used in *Sonnet for lost lasts* is a phrase used by writer, Susan Carland. The Venn diagram form of the poem *Catch: a break* was inspired by Brian Bilston's poem *At the Intersection*. The epigraph quoted in *The terminal velocity of raindrops* is from "Harvesting of kinetic energy of the raindrops" by Chamil Perera et al, in The International Journal of Mathematical, Computational, Physical and Quantum Engineering, 2011.

I am grateful for Dr Gina Mercer's and Esther Ottaway's excellent feedback and suggestions on the manuscript. The reflections and comments of members of my Poetry Circle on many poems in this collection are also much appreciated, as is the encouragement from Oasis Women Poets and the broader Tasmanian poetry community. I'd also like to thank Liz Winfield, Ralph Wessman and Jane Williams for their unwavering support of my poetry over the years. I'd like to thank the members of the creative writing group I facilitate at The Hobart Clinic for sharing the inspiration and healing properties of poetry with me.

I am grateful for the support of my talented friend Jen Lorrimar-Shanks who kindly and skilfully designed the cover, and to Penelope Clark for allowing us to use her beautiful leaf photo.

Much gratitude goes to my mother, my sister, our child health nurses and my friends Jen, Pen, Kelly, Sarah, Inga and Sally for their support during those challenging early years of being a stay-at-home mother with a husband who was frequently away for work. This book is dedicated to my wonderful husband, Jeremy, and our children Katie and Rory, for bringing love and joy into my life and sharing the journey.

About the author

Susan Austin is a poet, eco-socialist activist and occupational therapist. She facilitates group programs, including a creative writing program, in a mental health clinic in Hobart. Her first poetry collection *Undertow* was published by Walleah Press in 2012. An earlier version was awarded First Commended in the Best First Book category of the IP Picks 2011 competition. Susan was awarded a Career Development Grant by the Australia Council for the Arts to complete a verse novel centring on a theme of infertility, published as *Dancing with Empty Prams* by Walleah Press in 2023. This book was longlisted for the Tasmanian Literary Awards, Tim Thorne Poetry Prize in December 2024.

Susan won First Prize and Highly Commended in the Fellowship of Australian Writers Tasmania Poetry Prize in both 2023 and 2021 and was Commended in the Woorilla Poetry Prize 2021. Susan has been a guest performer at various writers' and poetry festivals. She has judged the WILPF Eve Masterman Peace Poetry Prize, been featured on Radio National's Poetica program and participated in a Poets and Painters Exhibition at the Bett Gallery in Hobart. She has been widely published in anthologies and journals including in the Australian Poetry Anthology 2023. She can be found at www.susanaustinpoetry.com.au and as *Susan Austin Poet* on Facebook.